LIFE IS
NOT A
STRANGER

HELEN VAN ROOIJEN

Other Books by This Author

Rendezvous at Loch 6
Rendezvous in the Red Centre
Rendezvous with Death
Silence of the River

Coming soon…
Silence of the Mansion

DEDICATION

For Martin

....

ACKNOWLEDGEMENTS

'**Life is not a Stranger**' has been an interesting book to compile. It is a lifetime of my poetry, my thoughts and a belief in the future It includes some of experiences, in fact many of the odd things that have happened to me over time. Things, such as described in 'Rendezvous' (Port Lincoln) and 'Roman Soldier,' (London) did occur and I can't explain them – except in poetry. That's all right and I accept it as the words have demanded to come off my pen – or latterly, into my computer. Ecology is important, and the state of the world, the same to me.

I love the River Murray and spent many months there as a child, returning as an adult, and finding my feelings and impressions haven't changed.

My father used to look to the stars with me, laying on the back lawn, when I was a child. He began my fascination with space and time, and yes, I was a 'Trekkie'. Later I studied as much as I could digest and understand of the components of science in that field.

Other things like travel, being an ambulance volunteer, nursing, plus a degree in Social Work then working in that field, gave me experiences that found their way into my poetry. Family and especially places, ditto.

I am deeply indebted to my husband **Martin van Rooijen's** wonderful artistic rendering of my wishes for this cover design, as he had done previously for all my books, and to **Aileen Pluker**, who worked her way through my poetry pieces to assist with this final product. **Mary Gudzenovs** is a magic computer worker in setting up and putting together my books. Thank you to all.

PROPER BAY MORNING

Wind withering and tee-trees hushing;
first draft of dawn.

Pitted limestone juts platforms
ragged to the sea
and mangrove roots steeple
a haven to shallows' fish sprats.

Shags stretch cold morning bodies
in ritual to the rising sun
and three black swans lift
flee low
wing to white wing tip -
muted calls ebbing,
long thin shadows
merge silver to the sea.

Ancient fish trap skeletal stones
poke bent fingers,
that curve out to sea
catching nothing now
but tides –

timeless green waters
and passages

that no one remembers.

MEMORIES OF THE MURRAY MEN

i

Plucked from dreams   of Tobruk and mortars
by the night bell clanging for the ferry
the punt keeper grumbled   stumbled from his bed
to light his first smoke
and cough his way down to the river,

a four year old girl   one night
I shivered   and dressed in my overalls to follow.

As uncle cranked up the oily punt diesel
I struggled to swing open the ferry gates
for the doctor's car to fume   and fret smoke
down the wooden ramp   to board.

On the return across the wide Murray
as the slow phu   phu   phu took
us back on the dripping steel cable
he'd laughed   opened his army greatcoat
and warmed our dawn journey home.

ii

The one eyed cook at the Wellington pub
rough chopped turnips   for the stew
and apples for his pies   with the same
great knife he'd gutted the callop at daybreak.

His pies wore sweet   buttery   yellow pastry
but he cored the apples   more in his imagination;
the hard bits and pips snagged teeth
and sent the boss's wife into tempers.
He'd off to the bar mid morning
"fer a drink for us both"   and come back
wiping his mouth at his elbow shirt sleeve
his lips trembling for his pint of port.

He'd bring me a squash of real lemon juice
with rainbow rings of cordial   seeping up
from the bottom of the glass   and I'd try
and try   to sip the colours   one by one.

iii

The old fisherman   lifted his drum net
from the deep water   beyond the willows
brimming with bronze fat callop
and green blotched cod   taken illegal,

the inspector bloke's not around
in the dawn   before the heat.

He'd row back across the Murray
brown summer   sluggish waters
slung low beneath his oars
pull   grunt   oarlocks clunk
hiss of water
bubbles rise from deep dipping blades
rest   and pull again.

Talk your leg off for hours   he would
at the bar   as the years went on   about
the state of his river now   and why
and how to fix it.

He'd frown   cuss them there up river
the drought   and water wasted in open channels
all about dollars   he's insist
and them   who didn't care about his river.

Then he'd strum his hand down
his grey bristly chin   grunt
and chortle a wink

and the beer level at his elbow would sink
ever lower   drying out   like the waters.

RING AROUND THE MOON

'Dufken' sailed this morning

Dutch scout ship replica   slow
slipped out through the northern entrance
towards night   and cliffing Althorpe seas.

The moon   near full   rides above

in a tatty spider's web of hazy cloud
ice crystals a huge ring   circling
arm widths across the sky.

In pitching   dirty   cross current seas

tarred sheets slap the mainsail,
the galley fires gone out
and water slops in wooden buckets.

The moon   cold   eerie within its ring

seeps ancient omens into sailor's minds:
a green meteor slices the ring

and *'Duyfken'* shrinks into its oaken shell.

BEACH

Along the winter wind-swept beach,
where gut-bellied gulls whimpered in the wind,
and petticoats of foam swirled loops
of lacy kelp into patterns   I walked.

My footprints followed in ragged
and playful determination,
but the time-waves swirled over
erasing my steps   my existence

and left the beach as before.

NIGHT AT ANCHOR

Waves wallow towards us
in uneven rounded swells

sheets slap   and slither against the mast

and a scattering of evening gulls
hasten the night.

Blue spirals to indigo
brings out a glutton of stars

and an enigmatic   glop glop glop
of unseen origin lurks
and waits
beneath our hull.

FISH

What teeth!

A predator   barracouta
King hake perhaps?
Out of place
amongst the slippery herring.

Were you gorging   surprised   netted
trapped   or caught as someone's line prize?

I rather think you'd go well   baked
with wine, lemon, onions   even garlic.

Some would say chillies   and insist
on mountains of horrid green coriander

but then
you'd be drowned   a second time.

CHRISTMAS SAILING

A ship sailed this morning
gunnels low with golden grain

and   leaving

in Christmas farewell
a blue and silver twisted tinsel streamer

unwinding

  slowly across the bay.

BONES ON THE SHORE

She stood
a lone figure

on a silken dawn shoreline
at   ebb tide

ventured a toehold
of weedy water   inbound
to slope out again
as though it owned the beach.

It did

and it cast out   bones
of a young Pacific Gull
white   translucent almost
perfect and fragile

to wait hidden in sand
above the tideline
for her to find

and give to a friend.

GALAXY

Last evening   after sunset
we walked the long beach.

No moon

surf and tides silenced
by stars   mirrored for an instant
in the back-wash sea slick.

Galaxy   tipped on end
no end   more visible
thumb prints

smudges   of light
in endless space.

GREEN TIDE

I lie back and let the green
engulf me.

Taste the green   salt water
on lips and throat.

Feel the cold flowing up from the south
warmed only by distance and a spring sun

the rush and pluck of great seas beyond.

Feel the smooth and sharpness of sand and rock
beneath my body   my feet catch
sway with the waters.

Hear the song of the waves   the tickle of weed
crackle and snap of tiny creatures
the swing and swish   of water across rock.

I sit up   glad that I can
green water cascades out of my hair
down my back   returns to the sea.

Green water in brown canyons of rock
a place of reflection

of decisions…

WINTER INTERVIEW

Scars   ridges   shadows
on her bleak landscape face
her eyes   shrouded   covert
seeking   but giving
and expecting   nothing.

On my desk the first almond blossom
sprigs of spring   fragile amid
the realities of her abused life.

Existence of abandonment
violence   transience
prisons   drugs   incidents
blurred inward
into her desolate self.

'It's winter. They're not real'
she accused.

She left   blossoms in hand   options
my caring   despairing
protection
and all assistance offered.

Who could know   if
the blossoms were discarded
bruised   crushed   or winter influenced
by a glimmer of spring   or   hope.

I cannot look for petals   in the rain
until   she is ready
for change.

TANIA'S HAIR

(1969 – 2000)

Tania

vital and glowing.

I followed you
into the theatre   last night,
watched strangers' impulsive hands
reach to touch your hair.

long curtain of red-spun
gold silk   a tapestry
of cirrus clouds
spread and flowing at sunset.

today I learned your hair
is gone   shorn   sacrificed
to chemo and leukemia.

Tania
no gods could ask for more.

TICKET TO THE HOSPITAL BALL

Yesterday, in a cardboard box
I found a ticket stub
with a piece of doggerel
I sent home in mute appeal.

"I've just been sold a ticket
Two pounds a double, not bad the price
To visualize the gliding couples,
Of lace cascading to the floor,
And satins whispering in colours
Of delicious hue.
To hear the band, and the bag-pipes -
For 'tis a Highland Ball,
Will pipe the way to supper
And add the stirring tartan to the scene.

While I, like Cinderella, must sit at home,
In melancholy self pity and wistful thoughts -

For vanity has no long dress to wear."

Mum took pity:
sent me ten bob for my hair

and I borrowed a dress
that had been presented
to the Queen.

GENUS PROTEA

Tough

as the continent that spawned them
flower sunsets cast in bronze
spear- tips of flame and soot

hard, butting cutting edges.

I saw the genus first
in TV newscasts   where
people died in Africa for liberty.

Still they die from the diseases
freedom brought as trade.

Now proteas grow
In my dry soil   feel soft the breath
of sea-winds   and listen
to the parchment crackle of grasses,

sense the murmuring echo
of this land's broken past

and summon Homer's sea-god Proteus
to change the shapes and outcomes.

Waits

ALPANA - FLINDERS RANGES

Far off
the massive dragons wait
tails curled about stony plains
back ridges   sharp against the sky
night flings bracelets of stars above
the camp site quiet.

Bodies intertwined   the dragons sleep
through endless eons   breathe in the dust
of speeding cars and feral goats
sense black and white footprints
people   of now   and the distant past.

Water
gushes down their backs
to gouge deep creek beds   through red earth
to litter the gullies   shed flakes of grey slate skin
and pile up gibbers   for trees to grasp
against the next flood.

The dragon mountains stir
snort bush fires   into the north winds
shudder and rumble
ripple the seismograph pens at Hawker
to remind man   that the mountain beauty

is only on loan.

FUNERAL FLOWERS

Yesterday's flowers

'Good enough for a grave site'
the young florist said,
and bent to pick a posy of roses
for a trysting gift.

She grudgingly sold me the posy
and I took it to you

my trysting gift.

THE DOORS

She stood
before the brown door of her house:
already the world was closing in.
The blue sky behind her shrank
and day retreated -
fled to shadows.

Next door
the green door rang with music.
Laughter expanding out
through the keyhole flooding
the street with light -
beckoned her.

She stood
awhile drinking in the nectar
of life and hope.
Her key shuddered into
the iron coffin of duty

she slumped inside.

PRISON WINDOW

The bars across my office window
segment the light into hard dust mots
that fall screaming to the floor.

I know it screams, they say so
the men shackled here.

I try to set them free, for a moment
with memory, plans, time herding
and show them how to let the mind
run free
to fly through the bars
up to the sky.

But look past the bars
I say
look at your image on the glass
the real reflection
not the false colour
you tell me

see through a clear window.

You made it

where you are now   you live it.

MILLENNIUM MOON

Orb of moon steadily rising
weaves a golden   sea path

on green-blue cold
bitter taste of dividing waters,
and ties together the liquid sea.

The moon calms a fragile road
through stormy waters
firm enough to tread:

waits and calls
lonely for another human foot-step
and lover's embrace.

THE BEASTS

Over the hill she found the tracks of a mythical beast
one she didn't want to know about.

My sister said that it had been following her for years.

The beast treads as I do
footsteps in a parallel universe

not called for
never summoned

crippled beast of pain and self doubt

sister
you don't know him
not aware of his black being
his power

but I've begun to dislodge him
cut away my submissions

sister
beware his tracks

and enjoy your freedom.

NOT FOR THE CHILDREN

Last night   streaks and wreaths
of cloud lay across the moon and shimmering,
the stars held position in a milky way, turned for autumn.

Today   'Mum, what's war?' a four year old boy asked,
butting into supermarket concentration.

'Nothing', replied the mother   but
the child turned disdainful eyes on her   he knows.

He sees the news   sees the mean eyes and hard men's
mouths
sees the faces of children just like him   and despairs.

Tonight   I watch the sky   the stars   and hope
safety for our soldiers sent

The despots rattle the sabers yet   ever again.

Nostradamus saw fireflies over Europe and Asia

predictions for the recent millennium's turning

and I too have sons.

RENDEZVOUS

Mists lingered all morning
I remember

grey autumnal waters   cold
surge and brushing of weed
swans and ibis call   feed
in the sculptured merge   of tides and sand.

I remember
the naked native girl   walking.

She stepped between the sand flats
carrying a grass string bag of cockles
pink scallops   black mussels
from sea pools of a shore   further out.

Way further out   from the hum
of backwashing sea shells and murky grit
at my feet.

Stepping there   back through
a time - slipped silver web
that shimmered off pure blue waters.

She passed me
coming in from the different sea
from that drifting haze   to look at me   to startle -
then   climb the beach
to dunes and old midden banks.

Bewildered I glanced away

she was gone   brief rendezvous broken
imprint lapsed   fading.

I remember   and I am haunted.

ROMAN SOLDIER

I remember a   Londinium lane
as the summer day drew in
not the exact narrow place -
but I remember   the faded man.

He trotted in a military trot
javelin pike held up   on bended arm
eyes ahead under his iron helmet
shaded red-brown his tunic.

I could not see his feet
below this modern street
his sandals brisk   silent on the cobble
stones of a sunken   Roman way.

He passed quickly a flicker moment.
The guide gasped as he looked at me
Eyes wide she said…   'You saw him?'
'They say he sometimes passes…'

Will he ever rest   I wonder
his guard duty unrelenting
eyes trapped   looking ahead
in his own ancient time and place,

but must he   run forever?

THE TOY SOLDIER

Midway
on the Christmas tree he hung
wooden   colours no longer bright
and he'd lost his rifle over time

but the little boy   watched him
loved him.

He waited
while his sisters grappled
to take the golden angel
from the top of the tree,
the new tinsel   the silver balls
and the glittering figurines -

to pack them away
in their nests of boxes.

"Where's my soldier's box?" he asked.
"He doesn't have one," his father said,
"it's long gone… son   gone
since I was a lad."

They wrapped him in old tissue paper
that whispered time   and memories
put him   to sleep   to wait for next year

with the angel
who loved him too.

DUSTY MIRROR

Tears   blurred image
sweeping years away   hiding
life's wrinkles and voyages

the facets of years.

Window through a flowing veil
space and time   dazed,
wandering alone life's
smooth paths and rocky tracks.

A boat's wake is forgotten
by the seas when it passes
and the mirror soon forgets

the image in the dust.

CAPE BARREN GEESE

Prison farm.

Stately grey gleaners
follow the harvest

stand among sheep
picking segments   of life
left by the reapers.

Low lines of stubble   lead geese
to lake havens   reflections
tonal fire of sunsets

out of reach

concealed from men
in wire cages
behind stone walls.

Wings whisper power
decision

soft
the shadows   fly
at dusk
and autumn.

Seasons of geese

of men   ruled

by poor choices.

DAILY FINALITY

Lipstick smudge
sunset smeared on summer's rim
of sea and land

lone kestrel spirals
silent sentinel of the dimming land

last strike
potent bloody coral stain
spreading

night extinguishes day's
existence.

in that moment
I am cold and afraid.

LOST BUDGIE

Swaying in the wind
with the sparrows
on our fence by the muddy track -
green breast
bedraggled golden head.

  Lost budgie.

I stopped the car
and tried to catch it
before the hawks overhead
swooped and got it.

It flew, a pixie, a stray, intoxicated
by freedom.

I watched as the sparrows
dive bombed
and bright feathers fluttered.

We saw it again this week
still alive with the sparrows.

Free
a refugee
not caged …

PICK A BIRD - ANY BIRD

I choose   always the kestrel
Sleek   angular and powerful

But   in reality I'm a bloody pelican.

Large and awkward
with an affinity for fish and water
slow and cumbersome

much like me   but sometimes

I rise

to soar with the winds   and words.

NATURAL SELECTION

Two new holland honey eaters gathered
grasses and wool strands
from the back fence   wove
a snug nest on the deck in a pot plant.

Two eggs, larger than I expected,
laid and hatched   as the birds
whizzed past us   ignoring
unless we got too close   then
they buzzed closer   into our faces.

They carried honey and insects
each fed into gaping beaks   diligent.

This morning   one chick   tumbling
and calling   out of the nest   flapping.

The pair fluttered around
as it tried to return to the warmth,
fed the other chick   the killer chick
and barred the way back.

In time   it fell between the pavers
and disappeared...

EVENING IN MY WRITING ROOM

A blue wren

a boy all cocky in his azure finery visits
the pink ground cover   searching for insects

his lady follows   well aware she's dull
but her voice is strident

and he listens.

FULL MOON WHISTLERS

At night cock willywags-tail whistles
down the blazing moon

'This's my place' their virile boasting
echoes across the gully

'Hear me' they entreat the hens
who pretend sleep,
coy heads tucked under raven wings,
but listen as females do.

The magpies start up to outshine
the moon with their melodies
of love and boundaries.

Heads tipped back they carol to the night
overlapping the tiny willywag-tails
as they chorus the promise of rapture…

then the frogs in the water hole join
to make their own claims

and rid the night of sleep.

PELICAN

Like the pelican on the ground
I'm ungainly   confined by gravity
and life's boundaries.

But there   where the sea lifts
pushes up   aerodynamics of the wing
and tilted feathers sweep   I too
feel the wind as I spread my arms

and unbounded   I fly   words my wind
phrases   my wing tips   and a beak
huge to hold it all.

We fly…

BLUE WRENS

I promised myself
I would be better
when the blue wrens came
back to the garden
as they had last summer.

Today I saw their fragile shapes
by the bird bath
near the trees   a glimpse.

but can I keep the promise
that expectation
to overthrow the clamp
that held   my mind

and fly unhindered
like the wrens?

Fear remained
panic furthered by expectations

The tiny wrens
did not deserve my burden
and have no ownership
of me.

EARTH - MILLENNIUM END

Earth of fractured mosaic tiles -
ideological rationalization the excuse
for greed   and gods,

bruised soils,   smoky skies,
species gone and stolen children;
of intruding concrete footsteps,

through un - named graves
in joyless ploughed fields
of blood poppies.

Pure - the crystal black grout of space,
infinity between luminous galaxies
and star-gem tasserae.

Earth   blue pebble on a finite rim
awaits rekindling,   renewal
in glorious, rhythmic flowing mosaic of life.

CAPTURED MOMENT

Sitting there on the long beach
I listen to the waters fretting
watch a sea pricked white with sharpie sails

and fishermen working the shallows
for autumnal yellow-fin whiting.

I feel quiet pressures of the flood tide
a flow of time
my life's journey moving steadily

I sense I'm captured
flowing like the restless waters:

and a boat's wake is forgotten
by the sea   when it passes.

My grandchild runs towards me

she trills a laugh   seagulls scatter
quick footsteps trip   stumble
in her haste for life

I catch her and she wraps soft arms
about my heart   she is
my link to infinity.

My tides move ever onwards
now   onwards to a contentment.

LIFE IS NOT A STRANGER

The sun drops arrows of light onto the waters
and   patterns of autumn clouds
moves them around   like my memories
of life.

Hardly winter yet   but the past is dimming
keeping special   loved people at bay
held private   at arm's length
while time and distance   age and shadows
allows   begs   I discuss other stories
and my passions in life.

I revel in the wobble of the gangplank
linking me still   to the Murray houseboats:
the people of the river   who walked within my childhood
other stories   held away by discretion   anger
love   and wonder.

The sea   ships sailing away   out past the islands
have occupied my pages   birds and places
thoughts   the wonder of space and time
history   and the unexplainable oddities in life
beauty and horrors   capture me
demand to be written
within   a lifetime of poems.

DEATH IS NOT A STRANGER

1:

The crash cart rattled   to my bedside   already
I'd seen death's grim black face   on the night's glass
felt its hot breath   its sneering grotesque

But for an old grey man across the ward   at dawn
that shadow had come   for him.

2:

'Be with her now,'   the night nurse said, one calm
evening
'She has no-one   her people won't get here in time,'
I held her soft hand   boneless   already cupping eternity

'Please dear, open the window,'   her last words sighed
and she was gone   a whisper passing.

3:

Raging hungry seas   a fierce rip tide   pounding
grasping surf

I held a friend to save his life 'Lift your legs'   I screamed
gulping despair, 'I can't hold you much longer   ... have
to let you go,'
Finally, the seas spewed us both   onto the sands
unwanted debris.

4:

The prisoner's hard   snake eyes thinned
already twice a killer   he threatened
and the warden   guarding from the corridor
couldn't get in to save me   if the bastard lunged.

Talk yourself out of trouble   I was trained for that   or
shout
tear out his eyes   as my old Dad had taught me:
it had worked   once before   on the streets of
Adelaide.

5:
Ambulance years   a volunteer
old faces remembered   gentling life on last journeys
accidents   long shivering nights on roads   flashing
lights
anger at futility of the injured   dead   young faces.

Now   I hear the sirens   touch my shirt collar
superstitious habit
wishing the strangers well   and that the siren songs are
not yet
coming for me.

THE REMITTANCE MAN'S TABLE

The oak table seated twelve.   Old wood
smooth   shipped out with a remittance man
fourth son of an earl   unneeded   given
like Shakespeare's widow's bed   second best
like him   to begin the colonial family.

In the squatter's hut kitchen   perfumed with flour
and baker's yeast
the table floated with a dozen crisp floury loaves.
Baby softly at her breast   another played
a nursery rhyme of slurping jelly.

They clung together   in pain of call up   his
leaving for war
as the firelight   flowed across the table it calmed
a path
firm enough   to hold them   for a moment.
Aloneness trickled   down her face   waiting the
dawn.

Home   he leaned against the table   three years
a prisoner
his body bone thin   his khaki rags   a shroud for
his fallen mates.
Farming years   hot winds spared the ripening
grain
sheep in golden stubble.

Frightened   they fought   the roar of bush fire
smoke seeped her lungs
making her cough.   His hair   frizzled above
streaming eyes.
A child's swing   hung   a smoking crisp tyre

42

doughnut.
Mounds of broken timbers
all else   save shards of blue and white china
gone
into ashes like dirty snow.

        But somehow   dragged well clear
    scuffled   scorched
        and blackened   the old oaken table stood
sentinel
        for the ghostly population   of ancestors
        that moved   within the swirling smoke.

PURPLE

"When I am old I will wear purple"

I wish I had written that line…

I want to shout –
Yes – I will wear purple and know who I am –
but I want yellow and green, scarlet and gold.

I want to gulp clear waters and sparkling wines,
and let life's slipstreams flow through my hair.
Let me swim or sink – I still want it all.

I want to hold the stars, to feel them pulsing
in my fingers, to taste the planets
and burn my tongue on icy comets.

Let me ride the swirling space nebulae –
on waves of red and blue and flame:
to be engulfed in eternity

and not care when I am scattered
as ash and atoms.

Then I would know
I'm part of the universe

and wearing purple into infinity.

FIRST DAY OF A LAST SPRING

The sea runs slow beneath the jetty boards,
quiet pressures of flood tide
a flow of time passing
on this first morning of Spring.

I sat there   hunched
listening to the waters fretting
a sea pricked white with sharpie sails
watching fishermen work the gutters
and shallows   and faltering a coming lament.

The tides move relentlessly
dark glass of life dream's endurance,
dragging a friendship to a winter place
I'm not ready to follow.

We shared yesterday   briefly
spoke of seeing humpback whales
return again to Sleaford.
As she looked past me
glazed eyes inward to memory
her weary face smiled.

It's hardly Spring today
the clouds hang grey   like cement
plopped in ominous mounds
to an endless horizon

above a sea that's reached its full
and the ebb has begun.

MY MARTIN

In my eyes –

his hair has returned to flaunt his youth again

time a mere plaything

letting him dream the wood beneath his chisel

the paint to waft free on the canvas of his vision

without doubts and age.

STATUE

Khafre
stealing out from the torn curtain of time
in stone form

reign uncertain

did he kill his brother
juggle the succession lines
to wield together the double crown
of Egypt?

Builder of burial pyramid and temple
at Gaza
in a time of art and culture

visage on the sphinx

now
a statue to hold in the hand
rub the thumb against ridges of stone
to feel time flow backwards

I wish I had seen it
touched it

and felt its story of mystery.

NEFRETITI

So - they've found you at last.

Identified
your mummy hidden through the millennia.

At first you rested gently
in the Valley of the Queens, until
violated by the ancient robbers
you were reburied by the necropolis priests
in a side chamber of the deep secret shafts
that held the mighty lost Pharaohs.

The beloved wife of the heretic Akhnaten
you sat beside the king
the loveliest woman of your world,
and step mother of the golden Tutankhamen.

Retrieved by the museums
you lay ignored with the commoners
until someone recognised your face,
the way you were wrapped,
the position of an arm,
and decided you had been a Queen.

Now, they'll disturb you again,
measure you, test your beauty,

and take the myths and mystery
from your bones.

FEET

Acrobatic feet point skyward
male legs muscular and strong:
Troupe of Imperial China

coming soon.

No calluses on those yellow toes,
the poster shows just perfection
feet in clouds no less

six men balancing

a world on red lacquer chairs.
Tai Chi comes from China
the movements slow and perfect

but I see

legions of female feet bent
bound and thrust into tiny shoes
for men's delight and marriage

at their mother's insistence.

PEGS

Soldiers on the line.

'We'll hang out the washing on the Siegfried Line.
Have you any dirty washing Mother dear ?'

Soldiers like dolly pegs strung
on barbed wire fences - expendable
split and broken, used,
laid to rest or trodden into wet ground.

I wonder - did soldiers dream,
in the cold and gunfire, of steaming
warm wash houses and mothers
who would wrap them in sun warmed sheets
from the line.

MOTHER

I worried about becoming a mother
there was room in my heart   in my whole being   I knew that
but   and there's always   a but   when one wasn't sure
he was sure   about children   and I was…   but
I'd never learned how to   be a mother
from a mother.

I know   suspect   my mother loved me   but
I was just the reason   she could be free.
Not necessary   after wards
that was drummed into me   especially after my wanted brother
died   a baby   and others perished in her womb.

Held at arm's length   through her alcohol haze
I nursed her final years   but never got to know her
a pity   and I've tried now   to understand
to love a memory   without judgement   unconditionally
the woman   beneath the wrappings.

BEES

Morning sea   mists risen
coffee plunged and drunk
book idle
thoughts linger
on the passive infinity
of bird sounds.

A persistent humming
Closer now and near
new mists
a dark cloud moving
a buzzing fog   ready
to enveloped me

panic and flight.

Not just personal regard
of allergies

I fled in
a primal fear of

the sentient entity
of the swarm.

DISCUSSION

Tim Winton says   insomnia
is ripples of sand
on a night pearl   of moonlit dunes
draws him to memory
and comfort in a city   he endures

He's right
but it's grey sea waves

going on forever
yet butting up to crumbling sands
remaining inviolate

or it's wind in wheatfields
golden full of promise
and flattened as the dawn   wind comes

still awake.

VALE MIRKO

Mirko Franov 1947 – 2000

No moon tonight –

the prawn fleet slipped to sea again
black waters a widow's lacey shawl
lights spread along the horizon.

Last sailing they found you asleep
in your bunk blue-cold
rosary beads in your pocket

they took you ashore to find out why
then gave you back to your family
your people and your God's mass.

Another now to stand your watch
to cook your stew of prawns and herbs
wine and garlic for health

they'll talk of you - and Kali
waiting for the fish to rise to the light
nights when the stars hang near

and boats push through storming seas
but you'll rest safe ashore now
forever reunited with your son

vale Mirko…

ANT HILLS

In formation like red iron clad gladiators
chests bared north to defy the heat
immortal, Spartacus   against the thunder
and thrust of monsoonal rains.

Spinifex at their feet   are the fallen shards
of reason   as inside   termite blind
and burrowed deep against the light
a million feet build and rebuild their colosseum.

Time   the ever callous judge   clamours to destroy
with swords of storm and tempest
and fists of mindless human vandalism
to break the cycle of their eternity.

CULLODEN

In the eerie morning light
 I saw   before I was drawn away
 from a indifferent tourist group

kilted ghosts fighting   and falling still
around me on that wind whipped moor.

A lone bagpipe's distant keening   seeped again
like blood splatters   on bracken
and into trampled heather

and ravens shrieked the shouted Gaelic
the screams of dying men.

Silent and alone
I touched   the un-retrieved battle stones
that formed still   the lonely cairn
where that roll call wasn't answered

and my homage flowers paled and mourned.
I felt the call   the sour pain of heritage
Scotland betrayed,

Macalpine   crowned kings at Scone
  their battle stones remain there
and our ancient royal line is lost

The drums beat that distant day
it sounded for all the clans
and its heart's beat echoed for me again
in a swirling clutching vision
that morning in the mists   at Culloden.

I have resolved the call of Scotland   claim
no vengeance   only this earth I borrow now
where I stand   where my bones or ashes will be laid
and leave as heritage   this Earth.

I've planted trees   cleaned the sky and sea
the human race holds no dividing lines
for my children   or my children's children
on this finite blue globe
spinning   in the infinite black of space

HOMELANDS

I hear the call of homelands for, I too, am dispossessed:
my heritage lost in battles with Vikings, the Picts
and the cursed English in betraying annals of Scots history.
We were crowned kings at Scone of an ancient royal line.

Culloden, where in eerie morning air hazy kilted ghosts fight
and fall still on that wind whipped moor, lone bagpipe wailing
seeps like blood out of brackens and trampled heathers
and ravens croak the oaths of dying men.

Stunted trees whisper still the foul deeds done and cannon
shots thud into my heartbeats. Silent the unretrieved
battle stones that form a cairn, the roll call
remains unanswered, and pale flowers weep.

I have resolved the call of Scotland. Gone - lost and claim
no vengeance only the piece of this earth I borrow now,
where I stand, where my bones or ashes will lie
and leave as my heritage this Earth.

I've planted trees and cleaned the sky and sea:
the human race holds no dividing lines for my children
or my children's children - on this finite blue globe
spinning in the infinite black of space.

CHERRIES

He bites, teeth showing, into rubies
juice spreads along his lips
as he watches me
makes a moue and spits a stone

as I echo his actions beneath the trees

Our grand daughter grabs handfuls
of cherries fills
the bucket full   for jam
and jelly that slides through double cream

pooling colour like blood
dropping stones to the bottom of dishes.

Hobart skies   dripping clouds as nets
over trees decorated

Christmas festooned with fruit.

SILENCE

Before   the grunt of winter winds,
and   heavy rain thudding onto galvanized roofs;
an angry farmer   straddles a rainbow sky
watches cumulous clouds move
drought distance away.

Before   the first sweet birdcall,
in the dawning hours   when a fretting child
denies a mother's sleep   the song's a gift.

The stillness   of an old man and his dog
on an empty beach.

Between   the ebb and flow
the waters fret and pull   a sea picked white
with sharpie sails   quiet pressures of tides
below the jetty boards   but the sea soon forgets
a boat's wake when it passes.

The green streak   of a falling star
of galaxies spinning   when   night's dark face pushes
into the moon's peach breast   greedy mouth
mewing   until the sun hisses heat
and blue eucalyptus mists fade.

Before   a baby's first breath
the gap   between gunfire when a soldier's
fear sweat stinks   a child's joy   reacting to a
caterpillar
and as lover's eyes and breaths meet
before   the first kiss.

The moment   that instant   when death
reveals the next quaver of time's harp
and listen then   when perhaps   for all
eternity becomes   just
the sound of total silence.

FISHING AT STINKY CREEK

It's a real place!

A place where time and the waters meet,
where an ancient creek trickles down to the sea
a sludge   when it's parched and dry,
a flow   rarely.

And yes   often it stinks!

The weed slumps into smelly decompositions
where salt and fresh waters   and link   mix to
brackish
and slide together back into the sea.

But sometimes   fish wait out there
where rocky crescents push out to form a channel
where lumpy sea fronds   lie
in patches give them shelter

and watching   where the boat's cast their squid
lines   I stand on the sand
and cast my fishing line out too

They catch fish and squid   I see them!
The lucky ones!   I catch only the moment
not like my Dad years ago
who caught big fat flathead   out there.

Stinky Creek - smelly, yes and fewer fish
but as I stand   my toes curl and uncurl in the sand
my eyes and my being are filled.

I drink in the sea   flicking salt foam   at my feet
sometimes dolphins glide and play the waters
pelicans skim the sea   ride the thermals
and in the bush behind me
tiny land birds hide   and call.

World and road traffic noises are smothered   fade
as the Stinky Creek's music   festivals into me.

THE 'LINCOLN STAR'

A tuna boat is missing!

The cry
echoed through the town
and peaceful Lincoln woke;

and when the sky cast aside
its blanket of inky night   the boats
put out to search for one squat
white boat   for six men
and a boy.

On headlands   cliffs and beaches
people watched   waited and prayed
anxious faces turned seaward.
A flare?   No, a shooting star!
and a quickened pulse   relaxed
reluctantly.

Night after raging night   day
after day   of pitching into grey seas
the boats of the fleet
searched for a glimmer of light
or a flash of white hull and mast.

Nothing   only empty seas
and the ships turned home
to shrug their failure
to waiting faces.

For months   they watched the sea
while polling tuna or at the wheel
for some sign of a friends' passing

and then
on a far Coorong beach
a lifebelt was found   alone   lost
the name in faded letters

"Lincoln Star".

BOSTON BAY – ONE WINTER MORNING

The sea was silver
so calm
that the island stood out in dark relief

trees
black calligraphy strokes   on the ridges
and along the low coastline that reached out
to enclose the bay.

It couldn't last.

The harbour pilot
weather charts in hand
still tapped the glass for confirmation

reached for the phone to warn the huge bulk
carrier
standing out behind the island

to give himself more sea-room.

ENIGMA NEAR AN EDGE

Shapes unclear hover,
demeaning my essence -
are the edge of my panic.

Desperation invades as I try to return,
held in a grip so intense
the dark void is physical;
shuts down my reason.

Unclear mind-set,
time-set.

Edge -
I tasted death's tears,
smelt the diesel breath,
saw infinity in the grain road-train
and pushed to the abyss
swerved back to save that driver,
reluctantly,

but I still see a relief
from anguish and numbing pain.

Enigma near an edge -
waiting.

BLACK DOG

Beware
the black dog   hunching
at the edge of reason

enigma
black dog   pitch pit   black
waiting   always waiting

it invades my emotions
turning a sadness
to welling tears

in displays
that embarrass among friends
devalue among strangers.

CHANGE

Neap tides
lay bare secrets
then flow to the flood.

Changes, drifting twisting
curling as sea smoke
slip past,
surge and whimper.

Gulls on a lee shore.

Far glitter ocean swells
lines of silver sun,
seafoam and rainsqualls.

Winds of apprehension:
reparations for life.

Thoughts sigh,
resolutions fearful
to print footsteps
on uncertain sands -

landfall.

LIKE ELLA

(Ella Fitzgerald 1918-1996)

Morning
a wan sun slips
unheralded   above the horizon
has almost caught the full moon
and the land mists
holding the night.

Foggy tentacles ghost
and shroud the trees
tethers damp hills   the still waters
and chills the birds
from morning song.

Lone magpie
on a stark branch stage
fills its throat and
like Ella   scats jazz melody
down the silent valley
into memory.

'How high the moon'

BOTTLE OF RED

Fits eagerly into my hand
awaiting the long stemmed glass

cab sav merlot
rich generous   dark berry
vanilla oak flavours   so smooth.

'Current drinking
with steak and pizza'
the bottle blurb tells me

but this morning
I'm full of flu and tablets.

I pour   and the ruby liquid splashes
curls silken into the glass's belly
to flood crimson vapours
even my stuffed nose can find.

I inhale
and dream a dream
raise the glass to my lips
for a sinful gulp   a noisy slurp
and fling a glassful
of promises

into the marinade for dinner.

YELLOW SHEETS

How can you sleep on yellow sheets?   They ask.
Don't they bring elephants to your bed?

O my   I asked   O why?

Well?   Don't they rumble the pillows
 and tumble the sheets
and disturb your sleep with their big purple feet?

O my   I wondered   O why?

I don't have elephants come to my bed.   Not one.
My yellow sheets bring mellow fellows   but

O my I questioned   O why do you ask?

Rhinoceros and hippopotamus   and tall giraffes
they dance tippy-toes   on my yellow sheets
they sing soothing songs
all night long.

FENCED

Woman   disdainful as her red hat
blue rimmed eyes looking away
beneath the broad floppy brim
white sash meets dress.

Her disdained glance   a fence
perhaps against the world   as seen
too difficult   so she builds fences
to keep it all out.

Her fence needs a new paint pot
repaint job   make it rustic   different
to displace the loneliness   but she won't

too thin   and worldly
dress too white and costly
under that red hat
she's knowingly fenced   herself out.

GET THE WASHING IN

Time to get the bloody washing in
I couldn't care if it stayed out and rotted really
fold the sheets and pillow slips
stack them in the basket.

Today's paper says that women cook for three
years
of their lives
Yeah!   right and the rest!

Snake   a big one   comes towards me on the path
I contemplate mortality   for an instant
step barefoot aside and watch it pass
down into the barbecue area and the scrub.

There's McNaught's Comet due tonight
in the west   bigger than Halley's
so the same paper says   rather
I want to see that!

Get the washing in…

PS :

I saw the comet
Low above the western wind farms

just an exclamation point   against the observers'
chatter

another brown snake met me today
it twisted and snuck into the groundcover by the
line

maybe I should give up washing…

BLACK STONE

The stone I hold smells cold   old.

Triangles of sharp irregularities fit
into the hand   edges biting   cutting

Browns and golden reds   the evening last rays
caught on the horizon   seep out
demand an age.

Questions   a knowing…

Were your primal atoms from this earth
Or   born in universal chaos?

Did you wander
as a seed meteor   across the galaxies
as the earth heaved and twisted
spewed out lava   while the planet caught
the moon   then hung it close enough
to force the mantle to a frenzy?

You became
geological dendrites fanning
from volcano depths to   as you are now
cold patterns shaped
like fossil fronds pressed   within rock folds

as if time   had stitched a blanket seam.

COLOUR SLIP

Brush drift of waters
on a child's primary palette

passages   of deep tidal wash
storms the island
seas of duplicity

colour-slip

dye tints
so consumer sweet
they glitz the senses   sensibilities
slur my integrity

sham political rhetoric
ecology lapses

my comfort zone   violated
by colour-slip lies

false flowers   a handprint
of yellow decay
rock shoulders slick slime

gulls shriek my protest

reality and time denied

colour-slip.

TIME LORDS

We were given brooms
to sweep the scattered rubbish.

Before long   standing in the cold
of infinity and time and space   we had swished
the universes before the brushes.

Swirling galaxies   of dying stars
throbbing pulsing quasars   event horizons
into black holes   mysterious black spaces
the still radiant nebulas   dead planets
and all the comet wanderers
until   there was nowhere to hide the debris.

And as before   we had to pile it up
into glowing heaps   waiting

to start again.

HUMS THE BACKWASH – OCEAN JOURNEY

Last night the sea slept well
dreamless   bed linen barely ruffled.

In dawn's mirrored silver
tides stir silky ripples   and play
kissing games with a lone dolphin

rolling slow hissing troughs
and tugging vees on satin ocean sheets.

Off Thistle Island

A pelican dips a pouched bill into infinity
scoops plunging silver streaks

**and gulls reflecting blue waters
under breast and wing   sky-wheel and turn
gathering light as sapphires.**

Dolphins come back
to play the anchor chain
vanish   as a shadow shreds
          the sun-fingered depths

I clamp the railings   inhaling fear
my oneness has an edge of vulnerability.

Dolphins   like silver needles
stitch together fraying threads
and tangles   of creaming bow waves
tack patches and drifts of biting spray

white caps arch purple
colour-slip green
rain ribbons weave storm curtains
and merge bluster cloud   to endless grey

then   dolphins ride before our keel
and safely sew the ocean-seams
to home.

VISITORS

Signatures
slanting to the right
the loops fashioned of the age

Blotted   scuffed inks
but I can read
Ridley – Gallagher – Ramsey – Burton
Cook – Quick – Jones – Price – Turrell
Thomas and Thomson – second cook
my mother's family name

the roll call so British

and hands that wrote them   long gone.

Thank you   Port Lincoln   they wrote
for this moment   to dance
to sip tea   to speak to a lady.

Ships MV Rothley   and Harpalycus

a steamer out of London pictured
with flags   hands shaking in friendship
crew from Captain to carpenter and cooks
Chief Officer and lesser ranks
faces   names.

'While you are dancing in ecstasy sublime,
Remember it may be your night aboard
Some other dancing time
So, spare a little sympathy
At this young man's morbid fate
Just autograph this symphony
Of your penitent Third Mate…'

They signed and one wonders what Rothley's mate
had done to be penitent aboard that night;

Someone else said   'They'd be back'

but did they pass through the war seas
that washed around the globe?

Marks on paper
Ships and men   marks blurred by ink and time
and old age   that sailed

and never caught up with them.

FROM MY DECK

1 am ...

Jupiter rising
trailing his moons on gravity leashes
satellite glowing shadows
of his magnificent self.

Runway lights
airport beckoning rectangle
enticing   bewitching
the paper planes   of my waked hours.

Like insects   they flicker flit   and float
eddying in enraptured   answering
mystical calls to swoop deliriously
into the maw of earth.

By 3 they're gone....

Landing lights burning great arcs
in the night   to flicker   flit   and flash
new fantasy trails away to the east
towards the sun and new day.

I am chilled by night's dew
and lonely.

Jupiter remains
his entourage again complete

no earth moon tonight to dim
his distant jealous glory.